The Official SUPER LEAGUE Annual 2012

Written by Neil Barraclough

Designed by Brian Thomson

A Grange Publication

ISBN: 978-1-908221-42-1

£7.99

CONTENTS

WELCOME TO THE OFFICIAL SUPER LEAGUE 2012 ANNUAL

Inside you can read interviews with some of the sport's leading players, including Sean O'Loughlin, Tom Briscoe, Kevin Brown and Tony Puletua.

We've also searched high and low to find some of the best rugby league photography.

If you want something a little different then head to the back for quizzes, word-searches and other fun puzzles.

Rugby league is an action-packed, entertaining sport – we've tried to make this annual exactly the same.

HAPPY READING!

YOUNG GUNS

Super League is packed with brilliant players – and some of the most exciting are the youngest men in the competition. Look out for these future England stars at a ground near you!

RHYS EVANS

Warrington, Winger

A Welsh flyer with strength and balance, Evans looks set to light up Super League for years to come.

JONNY LOMAX

St Helens, Half back

Acceleration, vision, passing ability and a good kicking game make Lomax one of the biggest threats in rugby league. Just wait until he hits his peak.

DARYL CLARK

Castleford, Hooker

Clark's twinkle-toed performances made him an immediate Tigers hero in 2011. Still a teenager, he could reach the very top.

JERMAINE MCGILLVARY

Huddersfield, Winger

A powerful, stocky winger with speed to burn. Catch him if you can!

KALLUM WATKINS

Leeds, Centre/Winger

Tall, fast, skilful and strong – Watkins is a Super League sensation and looks certain to be Keith Senior's successor at Headingley.

ENGLAND V EXILES...

George Carmont's try 45 seconds from time snatched a dramatic 16-12 win for the Exiles in the inaugural International Origin match. Carmont's score left England heartbroken after a pulsating match at Headingley in June.

Willie Manu and Francis Meli both scored first half tries for the Exiles, but Richie Myler and Joel Tomkins kept England in the hunt.

Tomkins' interception try meant England were 12-10 ahead going into the final minute, but Carmont struck and England were left to rue what might have been.

THOMAS LEULUAI

GARETH CARVELL

RYAN HALL

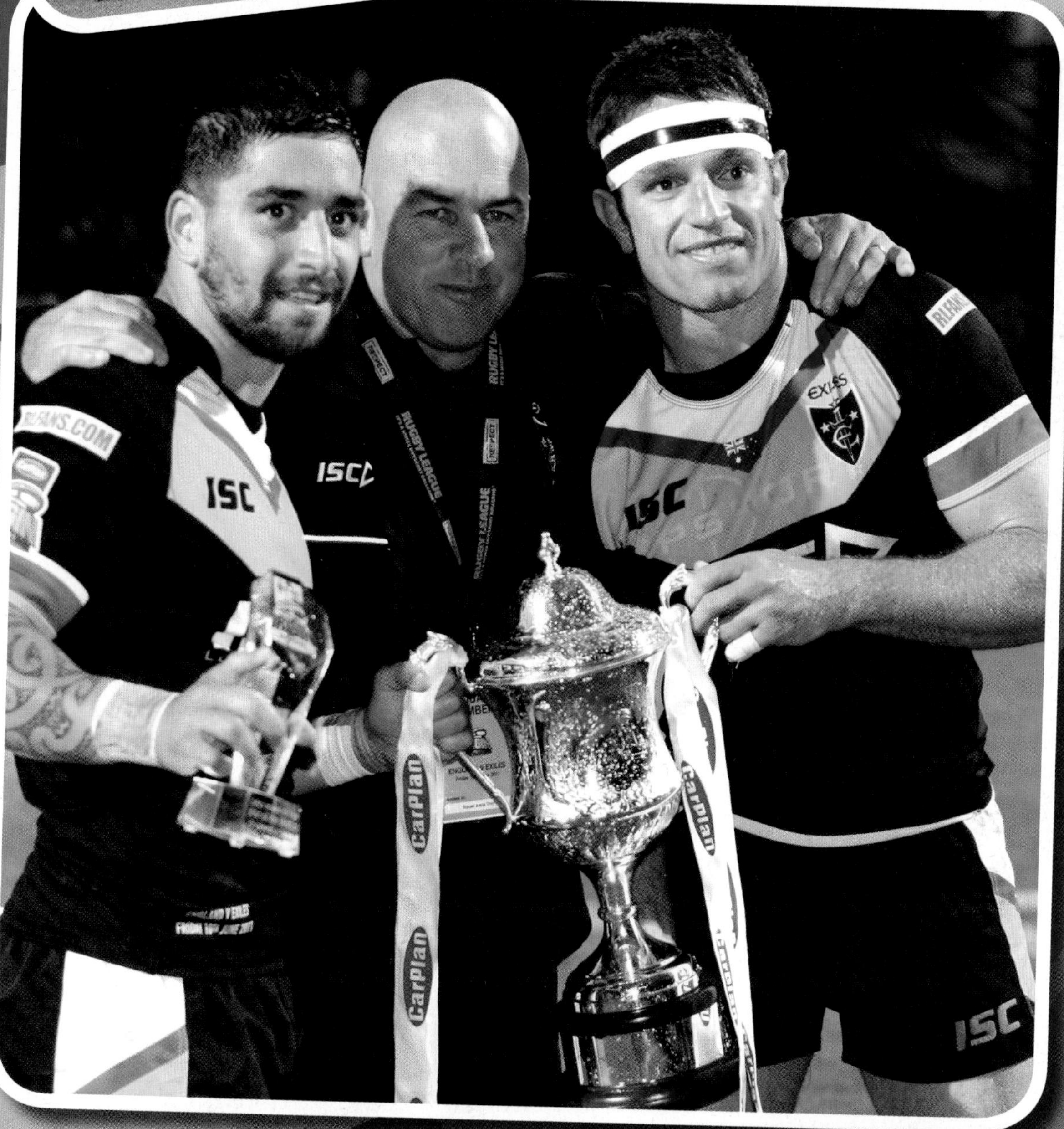

RANGI CHASE, BRIAN MCCLENNAN, DANNY BUDERUS

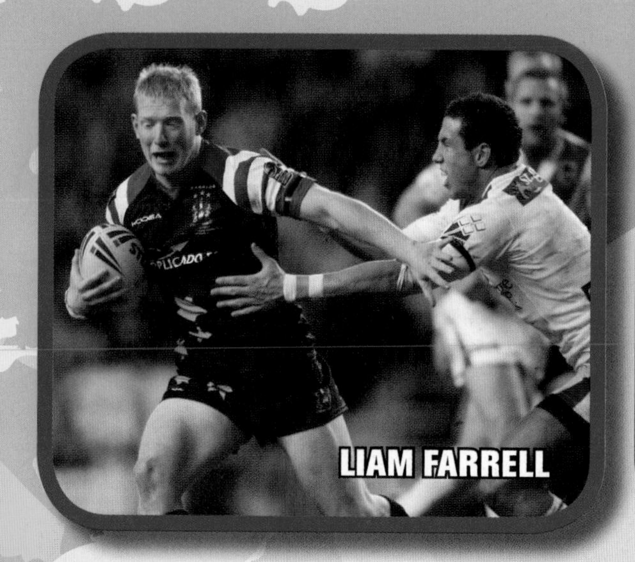

2011 WORLD CLUB CHALLENGE

Brave Wigan just missed out on becoming world champions for a record fourth time when they lost against St George Illawarra Dragons in February. The Warriors fell to a 21-15 defeat at a packed DW Stadium, but they ran 2010 Aussie champs St George mighty close.

George Carmont's try got Wigan off to an electric start, before Paul Deacon's penalty made it 8-0 after just four minutes. But two Brett Morris tries sandwiched Matt Cooper's effort to haul the Dragons back into contention. Carmont's second try and Sam Tomkins' drop goal gave Wigan a 15-14 half time lead, only for British hearts to be broken by Cameron King's touchdown and Jamie Soward's one-pointer.

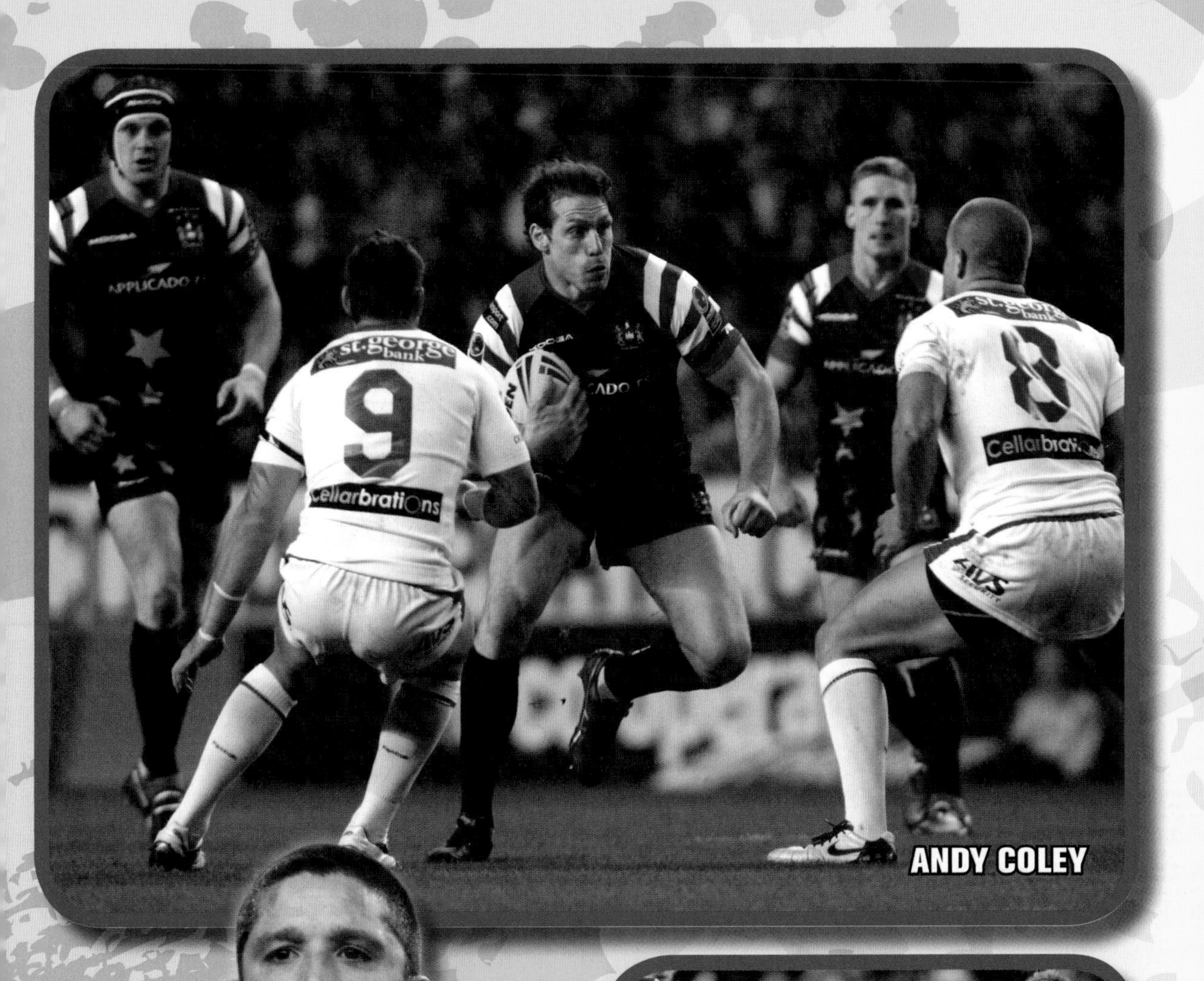

ANDY COLEY

SAM TOMKINS

PAUL DEACON

BEN JEFFRIES BRADFORD

Ben Jeffries isn't a film star like rugby league nut Russell Crowe, but he says part of the reason why he rejoined Bradford was to feel like a gladiator.

The Bulls half back started 2011 at Wakefield before making the switch back to Odsal in May. And he says the lure of playing in one of rugby league's oldest stadiums was a massive pull. "Odsal reminds me of the Coliseum in Rome," says Jeffries. "It's a fantastic place to play, the surface is absolutely brilliant and the Bradford fans are very, very good."

Jeffries was brought in by Mick Potter to be a calming influence to a young Bulls squad full of potential stars. Jeffries said: "I just want to give some blokes some confidence and direction. I'm 30 years old, I've played over a decade of professional rugby league, and that counts for something. You'll have good days and bad days, of course, but I know what needs to be done each week." He added: "Confidence is a massive thing in professional sport. If you can take confidence into every game you'll put yourself in a position to win 90 per cent of your games. If you've got 14 or 15 on your game, you can carry two or three. But if you're carrying 10 blokes then you're up against it."

Jeffries is now one of the senior players at Bradford, and is happy to take on a mentoring role with some of the club's youngsters. The former Wakefield ace knows all about life at the sharp end of professional sport, but he reckons Bradford's future is positive if they allow their young players to develop. Jeffries said: "When you're young you make massive strides. You'll see more improvement in a 20-year-old coming into Super League than maybe someone like myself who's 30. I wouldn't say I'm the finished product because you're always learning, but what you've got is really what you're going to have for the rest of your career by the time you reach my age. You'll pick up little things, but you'll see guys like Elliot Whitehead or Tom Olbison make massive steps because they're young and still learning a lot."

DID YOU KNOW?

A whopping 102,569 people crammed into Odsal to watch Halifax play Warrington in the 1954 Challenge Cup final replay.

BRETT FERRES CASTLEFORD

The future looks bright! That's the message from Castleford hero Brett Ferres as the club prepares for the start of a bright new dawn. Off the field the Tigers will be building a brand new stadium, while on it they've produced some of Super League's best young talent in recent years.

Joe Arundel, Adam Milner and Daryl Clark are just three youngsters who lit up Castleford's play in 2011. Now Ferres reckons there is even more to come in the next few years. He said: "There are a lot of young kids coming through into the first team, and we're starting to see the fruits of some hard work over the last few years. I think we'll see more good young players in the years to come. Talent from around Castleford used to go join other clubs, but we've made real progress on signing up some of the best kids around."

Ferres was included in Steve McNamara's England plans during 2011 and looks set for a future at the very top of rugby league. Tigers fans know all about his skills and talent – now Ferres wants Castleford fans to know how important they are to the club's cause. He said: "Things are going really well at Castleford, and I'm loving every minute. Castleford's fans are absolutely brilliant. They give you some fantastic backing and you can always hear them when you're out on the pitch. It creates a real intensity down at the Coliseum. The fans are not a million miles away from you, and that's great when they're cheering you on and giving you all their support."

He added: "The new stadium is also coming along in the background. Things like this take time, but it will be worth the wait in the end."

DID YOU KNOW?

When Tigers full back Richard Mathers got married, Leeds star Danny McGuire was his best man.

STEVE MENZIES
CATALAN

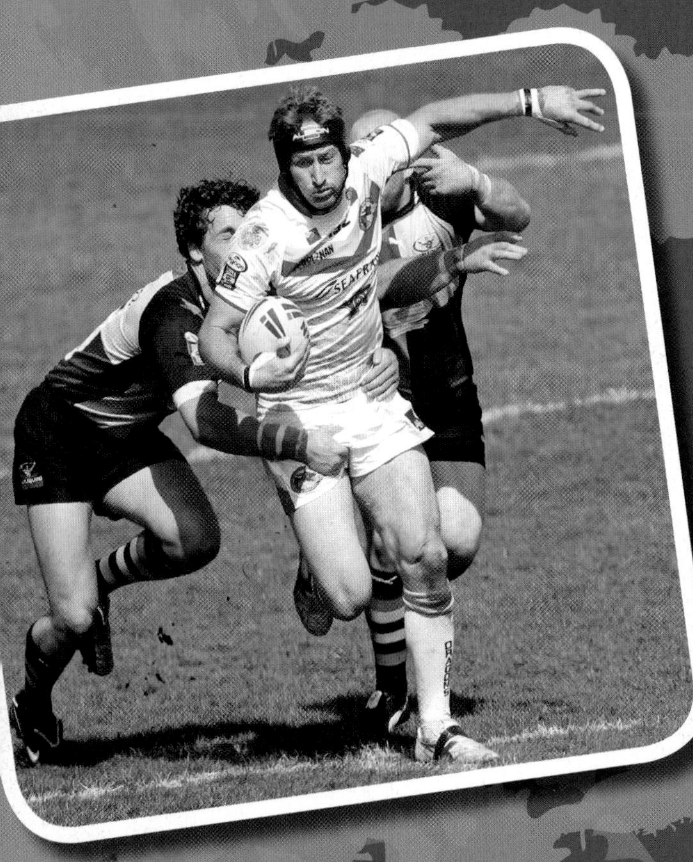

It's taken Steve Menzies less than a year to realise the importance of Catalan Dragons to French rugby league. And after one season with the Perpignan outfit, former Australian Test ace Menzies insists the future is bright.

He said: "We're perceived as rugby league for France, so that's a fairly big responsibility. Rugby league supporters across France look at Catalan Dragons, but the feeling around the club in 2011 has really been positive. The club's definitely in good hands and heading in the right direction."

Rugby league legend Menzies has left an impression at every club he's played for – and the Dragons are no exception. Despite being Super League's oldest player at 37 during the 2011 season, the former Kangaroos international still made his mark for Trent Robinson's side.

He even scored a length of the field try against Hull FC, outpacing England winger Tom Briscoe in a dramatic race to the line. He'll go down as one of the sport's greatest ever players – but the former Manly and Bradford star doesn't quite see it that way. He said: "I really don't see myself in the way other people see me at times. I just think I'm an OK player that's played for a bit, and I've played with some good players. I just run around and do some things on the field."

That laid back philosophy has paid off big time during an illustrious career. "I don't get too stressed out," says Menzies. "I'm just passionate about rugby league, learning new things and trying to be the best I can be."

He left Sydney club Manly on a high after winning a Grand Final in his last ever game for the club. Then two years at Bradford further cemented his reputation before he was tempted into a move to the south of France. Menzies said: "I spoke to Trent Robinson, and he put an offer forward. Perpignan is a pretty special place and the more you're around, the more you grow to enjoy it, embrace the culture, the weather and the way the French people live."

DID YOU KNOW?

Big-hitting prop David Ferriol has a softer side – he owns a vineyard.

CHRIS MELLING HARLEQUINS RL

Chris Melling never thought he'd stay in London long - but the Harlequins RL full back agreed a new two-year contract in July that will take him through to his seventh season in the capital!

The former Wigan and England man is still only 27 and has his best years in front of him, so his decision to stay with Quins was a major boost to coach Rob Powell and the rest of the club. But Melling says it was a simple decision. He said: "I'm looking forward to the next two years with Harlequins RL. Initially I came down here for 12 months and no expectations, but we've taken it step by step and my family's built down here. I'm enjoying life down here and I'm enjoying my rugby as well."

Quins endured a frustrating season in 2011, despite making a blistering start in the first month of the campaign.

Melling said: "We've done it in patches, but the fans want to see it for 80 minutes and we're trying to build a culture where we can do that week-in, week-out. Hopefully we'll push on over the next two seasons and challenge for that top eight spot. I suppose the club's going through a transition period, developing an identity and building a culture. Everyone wants results yesterday but these things take time and I'm just enjoying being part of it and seeing the young lads developing and coming through."

He added: "The amount of players in London playing rugby league at junior level now is pretty amazing. The lads coming through like Dan Sarginson mean it's pretty exciting when you put that with the rest of the things that are going on at the club."

Quins boss Rob Powell is now planning for the future, safe in the knowledge that he has one of the best full backs around. "Chris has been a fantastic club man since he's been down in London," said Powell. "On the field, he has had a really good season. We want to be a club where people come and want to stay. To retain a player like Chris in the middle of his career shows our intent as we move forward."

DID YOU KNOW?

London-born Tony Clubb scored four tries for England against Papua New Guinea in the 2010 Four Nations.

KEVIN BROWN HUDDERSFIELD

All aboard the Giants Express! Kevin Brown reckons Huddersfield is like a "runaway train" – and he plans to enjoy every minute of the ride.

Brown played for England in the 2010 Four Nations competition Down Under. But the Huddersfield captain thinks so much of life at the Galpharm Stadium that he was happy to sign a contract with the Giants until the end of 2015. Brown said: "It's like a runaway train. Since I've been here everything's improved – the fans, the off-field staff, the playing staff and the league positions have all gone in the right direction. We've beaten every side and we've broken more records than ever before. It's a great place to be." He added: "It's been a joy to be part of something special, and hopefully it's not going to end anytime soon. That's the feeling you get around here, and that's why I committed long-term to the club."

Brown's faith has paid dividends as Huddersfield's improvement means they look certain to challenge for honours over the coming years. The ex-Wigan ace said: "It's changed a lot since it was the Big Four. It was the Big Four and then the rest, but now there are a lot more than four teams who feel they can challenge and compete at the end of the year. We feel that if we play to our best then we can challenge at the end of the year. There will be a lot more than four other sides who feel the same."

A talented stand-off, Brown was named Giants captain ahead of the 2011 season. He said: "I'm really enjoying it, and the boys really help with their attitude. I'm not one of the oldest guys, but I've been about a bit now and I've got a fair bit of experience. On top of that, I don't think it's just me on my own – we've got a few leaders out there, which makes my job a lot easier."

DID YOU KNOW?

Luke Robinson had to delay his wedding after being selected for England's 2010 Four Nations tour of Australia and New Zealand.

TOM BRISCOE
HULL FC

England flyer Tom Briscoe says Hull FC's fans are some of the best in Super League – and he is desperate to reward their faith with a stack of trophies over the next few years.

Speed king Briscoe is now one of the most exciting talents in British rugby league. Strength in defence and fantastic finishing skills have seen the 21-year-old winger rocket to the top of the sport since he made his first-team debut in 2008. He is already a key part of the Airlie Birds' plans for the coming years.

But Briscoe believes the club's supporters are just as important as any player. He said: "The fans turn out week in, week out. They're a great set of fans. They get behind you and really push us forward when we need them."

He added: "I've played for Hull FC since I made my Super League debut, so I've got a very good relationship with the club. I love it here, and the boys are great."

Briscoe had not made it into the first team when Hull last won a trophy – the 2005 Challenge Cup. But he was involved in the club's 2008 Challenge Cup Final defeat against St Helens at Wembley.

Having already earned international recognition, the young whizz-kid is now aiming to fill up his trophy cabinet.

He said: "Hull FC is a massive club, and Hull is a massive rugby league city. You're either black and white, or red and white. They're very passionate fans, and it shows in the way they support their club." He continued: "Winning something for those fans would be absolutely fantastic. We got to the Super League Grand Final in 2006 and the Challenge Cup Final in 2008, but we haven't won anything since the 2005 Challenge Cup. They deserve to have something to cheer about, and that's what we're all working towards."

DID YOU KNOW?

Richard Agar kicked the match-winning drop goal for Dewsbury in the 2000 Championship Grand Final.

BLAKE GREEN
HULL KR

Rovers stand-off Blake Green is involved in one of the best half back partnerships in Super League - and he admits he couldn't ask for anything more.

The former Parramatta, Cronulla and Canterbury ace joined Rovers on a two-year deal at the start of 2011. His exciting attacking play was one of Hull KR's biggest assets during the early part of the season. Then scrum half Michael Dobson returned from injury and the devastating pair really began to click. Green said: "Dobbo has been a stand-out player in Super League for a couple of years now, and I get along with him really well. We enjoy our footy, we enjoy talking about our footy and I couldn't ask for anything more from a half back partner."

Green's creativity, flair and clever kicking game have seen him take his share of accolades during 2011. And his on-field success has helped him settle into his new surroundings extremely quickly.

Green admits he had never been to the UK before signing for Rovers, but he's taken to the English way of life straightaway. "I'm all set up in a nice little village called Brough," he says. "Even the weather hasn't been too bad! It was cold when I first arrived but that was a novelty in itself, and since then it's not been bad at all."

With his personal life sorted, Green has been able to focus on his rugby. "Super League isn't as structured as Australia's NRL, so you can play more off-the-cuff rugby. When you play in the halves like I do, being able to play what's in front of you makes things very exciting." He added: "We've got a great squad at Rovers, and there are plenty of characters knocking about.

We're all working towards one goal, and that's being a top four club in Super League. Having everyone striving for the same thing is a massive plus."

DID YOU KNOW?

Coach Justin Morgan collects designer shoes.

JAMIE PEACOCK
LEEDS

JAMIE PEACOCK crossed the great divide when he left Bradford for Leeds ahead of the 2006 season.

Now firmly established as one of the Rhinos' best forwards of all time, he's determined to carry on producing the goods. England captain Peacock, 33, has even set his sights on representing his country in the 2013 World Cup - which is good news for Leeds fans everywhere. Peacock said: "I've had a shortened season in 2011 due to my injury, and it's only two years until the 2013 World Cup." He added: "I'm going to play in 2012, and I want to play in 2013 as well. I don't see any reason why I can't do that."

Strong-running Peacock is renowned as one of Super League's toughest prop forwards. A tireless worker in defence, he leads by example and plays on where other men would have long since given up.

And it's that remarkable spirit that is now driving him to follow in the footsteps of other veteran players like Steve Menzies and Keith Senior. Peacock said: "Physically I feel as good as I felt four or five years ago. I don't feel any different to when I was 28 or 29. Until I feel any different, and that I can't do what I want to do, then I'll keep on playing."

Advances in sports science means Peacock now has some of the best brains around plotting his preparation and recovery before and after each match he plays in the world's toughest contact sport. He said: "There are a lot of players getting to their mid-30s and it's almost pushing up to the late-30s, whereas people used to retire in their early- to mid-30s. I'll just keep going as long as I feel capable of doing my job."

Leeds, England and rugby league fans everywhere will raise a glass to that.

DID YOU KNOW?

Leeds mascot Ronnie the Rhino stood for election in the 1997 general election.

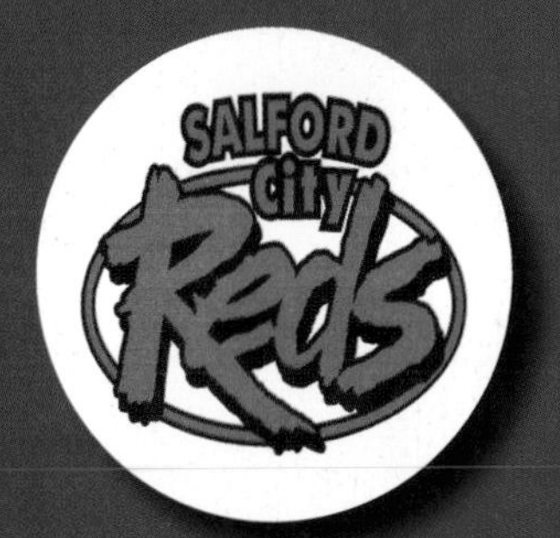

WAYNE GODWIN SALFORD

Reds hooker Wayne Godwin insists he's still young at heart - even if his team-mates already reckon he looks like TV chef Gordon Ramsay.

Godwin, 29, is 16 years younger than the celebrity cook. But spells at Castleford, Wigan, Hull and Bradford have given the Salford star plenty of experience in the red-hot world of Super League. Godwin says: "I don't know if I'm a bit daft or what, but the rest of the team all seems to see me as a young lad."

"They all reckon I look a bit like Gordon Ramsay, and they're always calling me 'leather face', but I'm never training with the seniors so I can't be over the hill just yet! I knock about with all the young kids at the club too, so that keeps me young."

Godwin joined Salford ahead of the 2011 season - their last at their old ground The Willows - and has a contract until the end of 2013. And he admits that the club's move to a brand new stadium for the 2012 campaign has got everyone excited.

He said: "You can tell the fans loved it at The Willows, but we need to move on and the club's gone to this new state-of-the-art stadium. It's going to be massive for the club, and great for the development of young kids in Salford. The location is brilliant, so we can attract a lot more people to come to watch us." He added: "It's great to be moving into this new stadium. I've never been at a club before that's moved grounds, so it's going to be new for everyone. It'll be great for those of us in the first team, but also for the up-and-coming youngsters who will be the future of the club. It's also brilliant for attracting new players to the club."

Godwin is happy to report he has no regrets about signing with the Reds. He said: "They're a great set of boys here and they've stuck together well. I'm enjoying getting a lot of minutes under my belt and I'm loving being here."

DID YOU KNOW?

Reds chairman John Wilkinson was awarded an OBE in 2005 for services to the city of Salford.

TONY PULETUA ST HELENS

There's an old rugby league motto that forwards win you games, and backs decide by how much. Luckily for St Helens, they've got two of the best big men in the business.

Tony Puletua and Louie McCarthy-Scarsbrook come from opposite corners of the world. Puletua, 32, was born in Auckland while McCarthy-Scarsbrook , 25, comes from Lewisham in London. But they're a match made in heaven when they team up for Saints. Now the pair cannot wait to get stuck in when the club moves into its new stadium in 2012.

Former New Zealand international Puletua said: "I was part of the last few games at Knowsley Road, and that was something special. To get the chance to be part of something special at the new ground as well is very, very exciting."

Last summer Puletua signed a new contract to stay with St Helens until the end of 2013. He said: "There are a lot of things happening at the club that helped make my mind up to stay. It looks like there are going to be good times ahead. My family is all settled in here as well, so it was probably the right thing to do. The family side of things is very important, especially when you have to bring your family half way around the world to be able to play. It's always helpful for the family to settle in first, because there are new surroundings and new people, but they've settled in great now."

Londoner Louie only joined Saints before the start of the 2011 season, but he's already getting used to life in the north. "It's good being up here," he said. "I've settled in well – apart from the coldness! All my mates in London are always texting me saying 'it's sunny down here, it's shorts and t-shirt weather'. I have to tell them that you need a parka jacket up here! But on the plus side, I've got fresh air while they've got all that pollution."

Off the field McCarthy-Scarsbrook is known for his jokes, while Puletua is a quiet man. But you wouldn't want to get in the way of either of them out on the pitch!

DID YOU KNOW?

James Roby suffered a fractured eye socket against Leeds in June 2011 – but played on for another 50 minutes before coming off!

TOMMY LEE WAKEFIELD

Wakefield star Tommy Lee admits he was "delighted" when the club secured a three-year Super League licence in July.

The licence means Wakefield are set to enjoy a place in the top flight until the end of the 2014 season and allows the club to plan for a brighter future. Staff and players celebrated together when the news was announced and Lee, who was the club's stand-in captain at one stage during 2011, is happy to admit he was pleasantly surprised.

He said: "It was a bit of a shock at first, but it's been good news because I'd already agreed a contract with the club for next year and now we're staying in Super League. You do begin to believe what's being said a little bit. We were the odds on favourites to miss out and we were preparing for the worst. We're just delighted that we've stayed up."

Now focus turns to the Wildcats' on-field performances, and with a new coach at the helm in 2012 after John Kear's departure, there looks set to be plenty of hard work ahead.

But former Hull FC and Crusaders playmaker Lee thinks the foundations are already in place for a successful future. He said: "We were already written off at the beginning of 2011, but we proved that we weren't as bad as people thought. We got a few decent results, and while we've had a bit of a slump in mid-season, I think you can put a lot of that down to injuries to key players like Glenn Morrison. Our effort's been there, and I do think we made progress as the year went on."

Wakefield chairman Andrew Glover added: "This is where the work really starts. We have to deliver everything we promised. We now have the ability to start building and strengthening the team, as players can talk to us with confidence."

Look out Super League - the Wildcats are on the prowl!

DID YOU KNOW?

Wakefield's Belle Vue Stadium was used during the filming of the 1963 Oscar-nominated film 'This Sporting Life'.

LEE BRIERS WARRINGTON

Lee Briers has had a fantastic last three years. First he helped Warrington win the Challenge Cup in 2009. Then he backed it up with another Wembley win in 2010, when he was also named as Lance Todd Trophy winner for his outstanding personal display. And in 2011 he overtook Wolves legend Steve Hesford as the club's all time leading points-scorer.

But the genius half back won't get carried away. He said: "All the hard work has finally paid off. People were always saying Warrington and myself wouldn't win a trophy, but that's been put to bed. We're now a club that's challenging for honours, but we won't get too far ahead of ourselves."

Briers passed Hesford's record 2,416 points during a 112-0 rout over Swinton in this year's Challenge Cup. He said: "Steve's an absolute Warrington legend. If I can be talked about in anywhere near the same terms as Steve, then that will do for me. When I finish playing I'll look back and say, 'wow, did I actually do that?' But right now I'm just concentrating on doing my best for Warrington for as long as I can."

Wolves have emerged as a genuine force under the ownership of Take That manager Simon Moran. And Briers, who is contracted until the end of 2012, is happy to acknowledge Moran's input. "He's put an awful lot of money into the club," says Briers. "Simon's a shrewd businessman, but first and foremost he's a Warrington fan. He's done fantastic things for us, and I can't thank him enough. He's the man behind it all."

But for all of Moran's input, it is Briers' own personal memories of that 2010 Wembley win over Leeds that mean the most. He said: "The noise that gets generated there is amazing. It was an unbelievable day. There were so many happy faces, from babies right through to 80-year-old men and women. To be in the team that made them all so happy will stay with me forever."

DID YOU KNOW?

Brett Hodgson was once dragged 15 metres and thrown into touch after Queensland forward Gordon Tallis grabbed his collar in a State of Origin match in Australia.

DENIS BETTS
WIDNES

They are Super League's new boys – but Widnes boss Denis Betts won't be using that as an excuse.

Back in March the Vikings were awarded a Super League licence that guarantees their place in the top flight until the end of 2014. That meant Betts had to plan for life among rugby league's elite while juggling the demands of a full season in the Co-operative Championship.

But he insists the Vikings will be ready to slay those who come before them in 2012 as months of planning finally reaches its conclusion. And the return of Super League is also good news for the whole town, according to ex-England skipper Betts. He said: "Everybody always wants a little bit of escapism and sport can provide that. If we can create that escapism with the performances on the field, and by getting the big teams here, and become a big team ourselves, then it gives a bit of passion and hope back to the area."

Betts last coached in the top flight in 2005 when he was in charge of Wigan. But that seven year gap doesn't scare Betts. He says: "The game itself isn't that much different to what it was 20 years ago. It's still about carrying the ball to a certain point on the field, while stopping someone carrying it on the other side. It's all about a willingness to do certain things right."

Betts' passion and belief is backed by the Vikings' chairman Steve O'Connor. Haulage millionaire O'Connor, the man behind Eddie Stobart, says Widnes' elevation into the Super League goes beyond sport. O'Connor said: "For the people in the town to feel that they are valuable is difficult – we've got some real social challenges – but you now sense genuine aspiration. When I first got here people thought 'Super League doesn't like us, nobody wants us there', but we've deserved our opportunity and I'm determined that our role is to prove that we would have been valuable three years ago. We want the sport of rugby league to look to us a model club."

DID YOU KNOW?

Denis Betts played for England in the 1995 Rugby League World Cup final

SEAN O'LOUGHLIN
WIGAN

Proud Wigan captain Sean O'Loughlin used to cheer his idols from the terraces - now he leads the Warriors out into Super League battle every week.

The England loose forward was marked out as a future star from the moment he made his first team debut back in 2002. Then Wigan-born O'Loughlin led his hometown team to Grand Final glory in 2010 to prove that dreams really can come true. "I'm very proud to be the captain," says O'Loughlin. "I see it is a big achievement. It's something I'll continue to be proud to do every week I get to lead the team out, and having blokes around you that could easily be the captain themselves makes the job a bit easier."

O'Loughlin has reached the very top of British rugby league, but what advice does he have for youngsters who have just been asked to captain their amateur team or school? "I don't think it's about trying to be any different as a player," he says. "It's about doing your job and trying to do it the best you can. Hopefully people can see you doing that. Being captain is a job I enjoy and I like to think that it brings the best side out my game as well."

O'Loughlin will be 29 when the 2012 season starts, and he is now firmly established as one of Wigan's senior players. But with exciting youngsters like Sam Tomkins, Josh Charnley and Joel Tomkins all committed to the club on long-term contracts, O'Loughlin says the future looks bright. "If you get those types of young lads playing week-in, week-out, they are exactly the type of player you want to cement their future at the club. That's what we've done and if you can do that, and they're happy here, then that gives you a great basis for the future."

Wigan start next season with a new coach at the helm after Michael Maguire's departure, but they will remain as one of the game's biggest forces for years to come.

DID YOU KNOW?

Pat Richards scored a try in the 2005 NRL Grand Final that helped Wests Tigers beat North Queensland Cowboys.

SUPER LEAGUE LEGENDS

ROBBIE HUNTER-PAUL

A flashy scrum half who played more than 300 games for Bradford, Robbie lit up Odsal with his dancing feet and brilliant ability. In 1996 he became the first player to score a hat-trick in a Challenge Cup Final at Wembley, despite Bradford eventually losing 40-32 against St Helens.

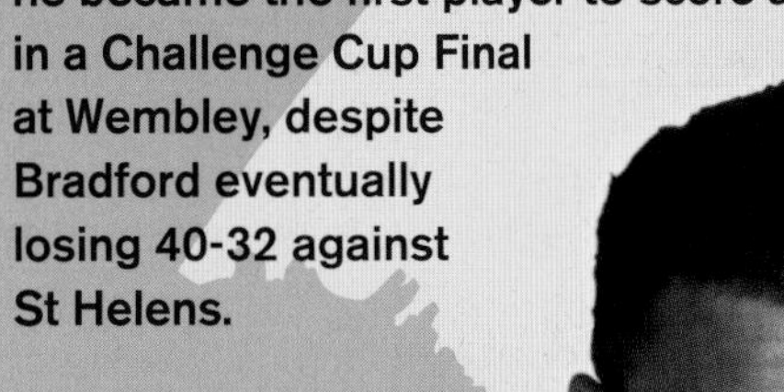

KEIRON CUNNINGHAM

Cunningham retired at the end of 2010 after 17 years with St Helens. He is one of rugby league's greatest ever hookers, and fittingly scored the final try in the final league match held at Knowsley Road.

He played for Wales and Great Britain, made over 400 appearances for St Helens and a bronze statue of Cunningham will stand outside Saints' new ground.

ANDY FARRELL OBE

Farrell was the youngest ever Great Britain captain when he was appointed in 1996 aged just 21.

A double Man of Steel winner, Farrell also scooped the Golden Boot in 2004 when he was voted the world's best player.

'Faz' was captain when Wigan won the first Super League Grand Final in 1998.

PAUL SCULTHORPE

'Scully' won four Grand Finals, three Challenge Cups and two World Club Challenges during a glorious career with St Helens.

In 2002 he rewrote the history books by becoming the first player to win back-to-back Man of Steel awards. He was named as the Great Britain captain in 2005, before retiring in 2008.

KEITH SENIOR

The towering ex-Leeds centre has played in every Super League season since the switch to summer rugby in 1996.

He started at Sheffield, where he won the Challenge Cup in 1998, before signing for Leeds in 1999.

A regular for Great Britain and England before his international retirement in 2009, Senior won four Super League titles with the Rhinos.

SPOT THE STADIUM!

Can you name these Super League grounds? We'll give you a clue for each one.

You won't find any Rovers here.

Be quiet! You don't want to make those Bulls angry!

Looking for fun in the capital? You might head here.

It's like a zoo here, especially with all those Rhinos charging about.

Whenever there's a battle here, there are plenty of Warriors on hand.

Is that a Wolf whistle I hear?

All Answers on Page 62

WORDSEARCH

Can you spot these Super League stars in the grid below?

Lynch
Arundel
Dureau
Sammut
Purdham
McGillvary
Briscoe
Dobson
Sinfield
Broughton
Wilkin
Widnes
Monaghan
Tomkins

V J M D G D M R Y B X Q X Y H G C C
D Z Q D O H W I L K I N N N G Y B X
W E L B W B Z W L B X X D P W D Y I
O R O D N H S F T S J R X L N M S K
B A T J M I K O J Y D E S A E X A W
R X T U T W L Y N C H N H D V Y M I
O T I X Z V U L Q C I G U L Q T M D
U M A U Y Y E S N K A E I F Q E U N
G J C O G D D F M N J U E E I A T E
H K V G N B C O O A H J S S Y S V S
T X H U I W T M I U I X I N R C Q Y
O M R G W L D U R E A U N M L I S Q
N A J H M O L J W I J C F S E N F H
F T T F G Z C V U Z K R I N S P K T
K V V A V Y B M A K H H E T M M E M
P U R D H A M D C R G C L N P O T H
K W M B E F A R S N Y N D P F P B I
U Z Q H C G I F B R I S C O E O J R

1. Which team did Leeds beat in the Grand Finals of 2007, 2008 and 2009?
2. Wigan are the only Super League club to share a ground with a football team. True or false?
3. From which club did Warrington sign Richie Myler?
4. Which Castleford player has a part-time career as a male model?
5. Who won the first Super League Grand Final? And in what year was it played?
6. Where do Catalan Dragons play their home games?
7. Who was the Exiles' captain in 2010?
8. Which city hosted the 2008 World Cup Final between New Zealand and Australia?
9. Can you name Hull KR's mascot?
10. Who kicked the match-winning drop goal in the 2002 Grand Final?
11. Which two teams competed in the 2007 Challenge Cup Final – the first at the 'new' Wembley?
12. Which Australian side beat Wigan in the 2011 World Club Challenge?
13. Which three grounds hosted the Challenge Cup Final between 2000-2006?

Answers on Page 62 & 63

SPOT THE DIFFERENCE

Can you spot the 6 differences in the pictures below? Answers on Page 63.

FUN FACTS

1. Jamie Jones-Buchanan named his three children, Lore, Dacx and Kurgan, after sci-fi characters.

2. Despite his name, Sam Moa actually plays for Tonga.

3. Ben Cockayne is an Iraq veteran.

4. Wigan's Paul Deacon claims ex-Bradford team mate Brian McDermott (pictured) was his worst ever room-mate – because he used to watch television naked!

5. Tony Smith used to live above a Fish and Chip shop when he played for Workington.

6. Olsi Krasniqi was born in Albania and took up rugby league after moving to London.

DOES SAM TOMKINS FANCY A NEW CAREER AS A REFEREE?

FEELING THE SQUEEZE! MATT KING GETS TRAPPED

THE HARLEQUINS RL'S MASCOT HAS FUN WITH A PHOTOGRAPHER

ST HELENS LEGEND KEIRON CUNNINGHAM HAS HIS LIFE TURNED UPSIDE DOWN

WHOOPS! LEE GILMOUR LOSES HIS GRIP

BLAST OFF! DANNY BROUGH TRIES TO GET THROUGH A GAP

RL GOES TO HOLLYWOOD

Rugby league is going to Hollywood – thanks to Welsh international and Crusaders star Gareth Thomas.

Oscar-nominated actor Mickey Rourke is set to play Thomas in an upcoming movie after hearing about the Welshman's decision to publicly talk about being gay. Rourke, who is also friends with Huddersfield Giants prop Keith Mason, is even going to have two of his teeth implants temporarily removed to help recreate Thomas' trademark grin.

As the star of 'The Wrestler', Rourke is used to training for physically demanding roles. And he even watched Super League's 'Millennium Magic' weekend in Cardiff in a bid to brush up on his rugby knowledge.

Rourke said: "I'm going to be as fit as a fiddle. Why wouldn't I be? I'm not going to disrespect the sport." He added: "I'm researching rugby league but I'm doing it a little at a time. I'm not trying to learn something I know nothing about all in one day."

Thomas, a former Welsh rugby union international and British Lions captain, switched to rugby league in 2010. At the end of his first season in rugby league he helped Wales to qualify for the 2011 Four Nations competition. But he admits he needed some persuading to agree to the idea of the film. Thomas said: "I did need some convincing at first, because I'm not proud of everything in my life. There are a lot of things that I'm embarrassed about, but I sat down with Mickey over several meetings and realised that he wants it to be a really strong, powerful message. It would have definitely been something I'd have regretted if I hadn't done it."

He continued: "I want Mickey to portray it so that when people walk out of the cinema, they've been through all the emotions I went through. If gay people can realise the world of sport isn't the world it's often believed to be, and if straight people can figure out how they can make things a little bit easier for other people as well, then that would be great. There are people in all kinds of environments going through the same turmoil I went through."

REFEREES

They've got the hardest job in rugby league. Making split-second decisions in front of thousands of passionate fans isn't easy. But these guys do it every week – and love it.

Can you name these Super League referees?

The answers are on page 63.

3
4
5
6
7
ISC
RFL
engage
Mutual Assurance

5 GREAT TRIES

Jamie Foster (St Helens)

Leeds v St Helens, 2011

Saints were already cruising to victory when their young winger Foster produced a stunning moment of magic to juggle the ball behind his back two minutes from time.

Kris Radlinski (Wigan)

Wigan v Bradford, 2000

Bradford led 19-14 when the clock reached 80 minutes, but Andy Farrell set Steve Renouf free inside his own half and Radlinski backed up for a brilliant try. Farrell kept his nerve to land the conversion and steal the points.

Leroy Cudjoe (Huddersfield)

Warrington v Huddersfield, 2010 play-offs

The Wolves were red-hot favourites, but Huddersfield produced a stunning performance in the 2010 play-offs. Cudjoe's 90-metre effort sealed a famous win.

Scott Donald (Leeds)

Leeds v St Helens, 2007 Grand Final

Rhinos were only just ahead in a tense Grand Final when Aussie winger Donald burst free in his own half and swerved around Paul Wellens. Leeds went on to win 33-6.

Keiron Cunningham (St Helens)

St Helens v Castleford, 2010

Saints needed to win their last ever league game at Knowsley Road by nine points to finish second in the table. Legend Cunningham went over nine seconds from time - and Saints won 40-30.

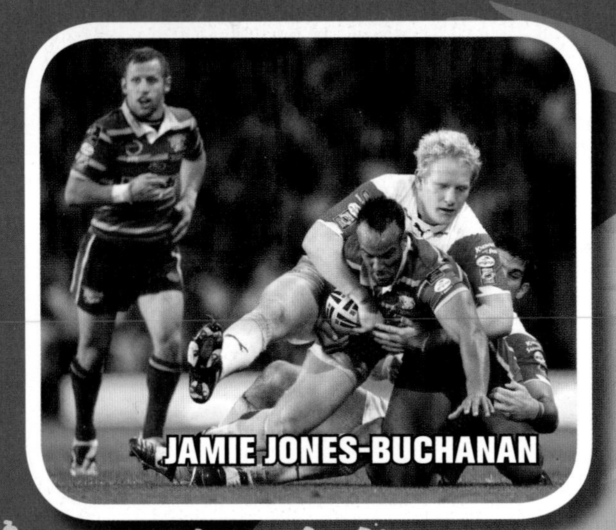
JAMIE JONES-BUCHANAN

ST HELENS FANS

GRAND FINAL

It started on a rainy night in 1998.

Jason Robinson scorched under the posts, Wigan won the inaugural Super League Grand Final and a spectacular sporting event was born.

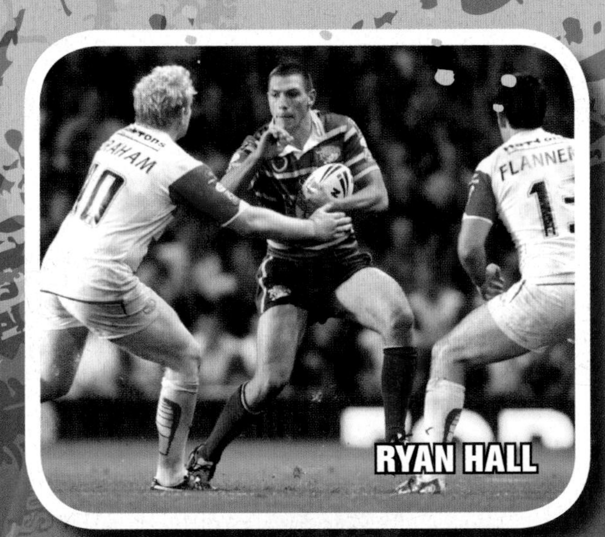
RYAN HALL

Now it's one of the highlights of the rugby league calendar. One match, one winner, one team crowned as Super League champions.

What are your favourite Grand Final memories?

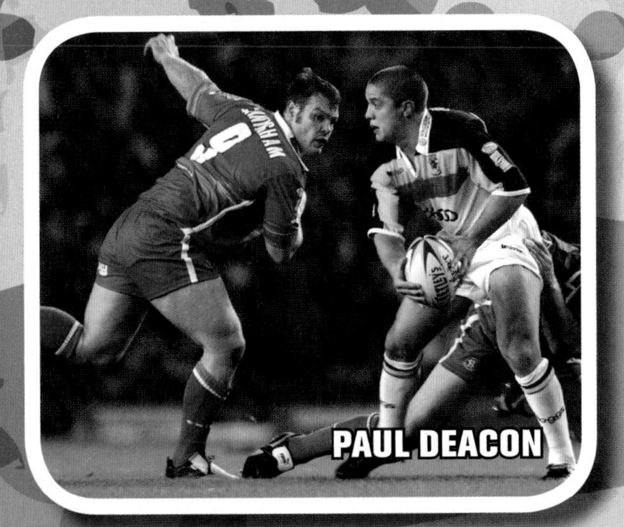
PAUL DEACON

MARK RIDDELL & THOMAS LEULUAI

WIGAN CELEBRATE IN 2010

WILLIE POCHING

CELEBRITY FANS

What do Johnny Vegas, Rio Ferdinand, Gethin Jones and Russell Crowe all have in common? They all love rugby league!

Comedian Johnny Vegas is a massive St Helens fan, while Manchester United ace Ferdinand regularly tweets about his love of league.

Gladiator star Russell Crowe enjoys the sport so much he bought South Sydney Rabbitohs, one of Australia's leading clubs.

And TV star Jones, 33, has even played the sport as well as being an ambassador for the 2013 Rugby League World Cup. The former Blue Peter host and Strictly Come Dancing sensation fell in love with rugby league while studying at Manchester Met University. He said: "I did a bit of rugby league coaching when I was at university and I played for the university team. I absolutely love the sport. It was so fast, ferocious and fair – in that it was just man against man – and it really appealed to me."

He added: "In some ways rugby league can be more appealing to watch than rugby union. The breakdown in rugby union can be very difficult to understand, whereas with rugby league you've got six tackles to get to the try-line, and that's it."

Proud Welshman Jones attended the 2011 Millennium Magic weekend in Cardiff, where he got to watch all 14 Super League teams play in just two action-packed days. It was an experience that blew him away. He said: "In rugby league all the fans mix together brilliantly, and that's something that might be unique to rugby league. If you go to a Challenge Cup Final, you'll see every club represented in the crowd, not just the two who are playing. That's a very special thing. Rugby league fans are fans of the sport first and their club second. That's what makes it such a magical experience."

And Jones is already counting down the days until Wales and England host the 2013 Rugby League World Cup. He said: "I'll certainly be there and so will my mates. We were born and bred on rugby union, not really realising rugby league was there, but that's something that's changing now and it's a brilliant sport to watch or play."

DRAMATIC MOMENTS

We all know Super League is full of action, do you remember these dramatic moments?

"It's wide to West" is a legendary commentary line from Super League's most famous try. St Helens' Chris Joynt finished a brilliant move after the final hooter to deny Bradford a famous win at Knowsley Road.

St Helens and Bradford were locked at 18-18 in the closing stages of the 2002 Super League Grand Final, only for Saints scrum half Sean Long to boot the title-winning drop goal. How's that for handling the pressure?

Hull KR thought they'd snatched a dramatic win at Hull FC back in July 2010. They had a three-man overlap in the last minute, but somehow FC winger Tom Briscoe got across and stopped Peter Fox with a brilliant tackle. FC took the points.

Gareth Thomas was Crusaders' biggest signing when he joined the club in early 2010. But the former Wales and British Lions rugby union captain soon discovered how tough league was - he got knocked out on his debut against Catalan Dragons.

Aussie ace Andrew Johns only played three games for Warrington, but he made an unforgettable impression during his brief Super League spell in 2005.

QUIZ ANSWERS

Spot the Stadium, Page 42

1 KC Stadium, Hull FC

2 Twickenham Stoop, Harlequins RL

3 Grattan Stadium/Odsal, Bradford Bulls

4 Headingley Carnegie, Leeds Rhinos

5 DW Stadium, Wigan Warriors

6 Halliwell Jones Stadium, Warrington Wolves

Wordsearch, Page 44

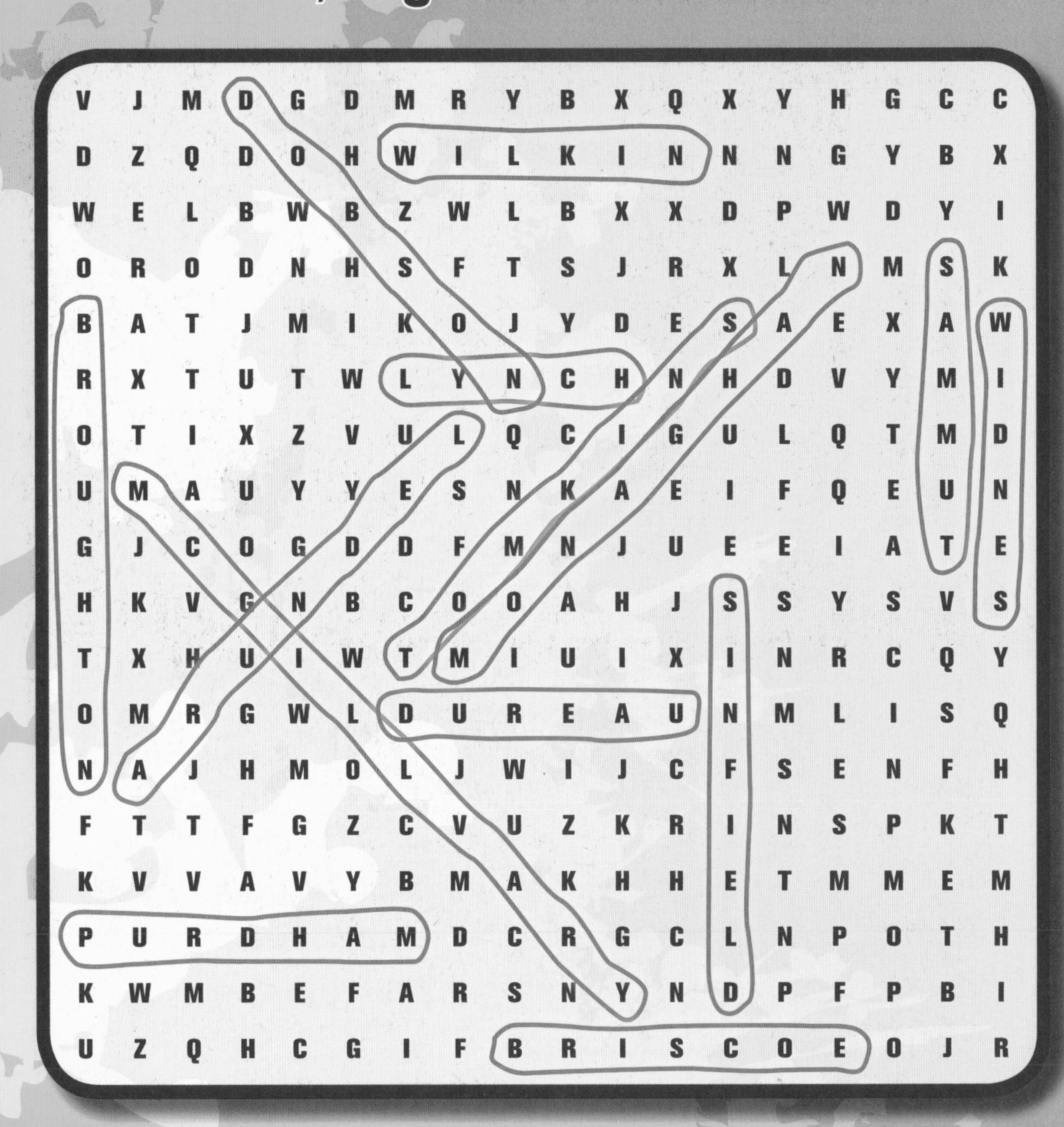